HIDDEN PICTURES

Larry Daste

Publisher's Note

In this challenging puzzle book, artist Larry Daste has concealed nearly 300 objects in 24 scenes set in Africa, India, Australia, and the Americas. Picture captions tell you what objects to look for. Feel free to turn the page this way and that to locate rotated objects. When you find them, you can outline them in marker or shade them lightly with a pencil. Try to find all of the hidden objects—which include food, clothing, animals, and maps of the U.S. and some of the states—before you turn to the Solutions, which begin on page 25. If you enjoy coloring, you can color in the pictures as well.

These West Highland white terriers enjoy frolicking outdoors. But they haven't noticed the 13 objects concealed around them in the yard: an **ice cream scoop**, a **whale**, a **shorthandled hatchet**, a **seahorse**, **2 carrots**, a **socket wrench**, a **crescent shape**, a **garden spade**, a **barbecue fork**, a **hawk**, a **firefighter's ax**, and a **barbecue spoon**.

The hippos didn't spot the 15 objects that don't belong at their
favorite watering hole: **4 hearts**, an **olive**, a **bird**, a **snake**, a
radish, a **pear**, an **ice skate**, a **map of Louisiana**, a **dog biscuit**,
a **safety pin**, a **fish**, and a **pencil**.

These elephants haven't noticed the following 11 things during their walk: a **fox's head**, a **squirrel**, a **jet plane**, a yo-yo, an **orange slice**, a **banana**, Robin Hood's cap, a **boxing glove**, a **fountain pen**, a **parrot**, and a **bowl of popcorn**.

The lion family seems unaware that 12 things are hidden so close to them. Look carefully for: a **backpack**, a **ketchup bottle**, **pruning shears**, a **peace pipe**, **bananas**, a **baseball cap**, **Swiss cheese**, a **toadstool**, a **hand saw**, a **slipper**, a **dinosaur**, and a **crown**.

These sea creatures are too busy to pay attention to 14 things in their tropical paradise: a **baseball bat**, a **key**, a **lifeguard's whistle**, a **shamrock**, a **boomerang**, a **cupcake**, a **bell**, a **caterpillar**, a **cotton swab**, a **rabbit**, a **sweatsock**, a **horseshoe**, a **cane**, and a **woodchuck**.

The sea birds can find the seahorses and octopus, but they can't locate the following 12 objects: a **pair of eyeglasses**, a **bell**, a **rocket ship**, a **paintbrush**, a **pearl ring**, a **bat**, a **wrench**, an **eel**, a **dinner fork**, a **moth**, a **pigeon**, and a **comb**.

The rhinoceros and crocodile have no idea that the following 17 objects are close at hand: **pliers**, a **bunch of celery stalks**, a **map of California**, **bananas**, a **cowboy boot**, a **flashlight**, a **chair**, an **artichoke**, a **screwdriver**, a **salt shaker**, a **muffin**, a **rabbit's head**, a **metal nut**, a **Civil War cap**, a **bat's head**, a **marching band hat**, and a **caterpillar**.

The charging tiger could find 13 hidden objects if it weren't in such a hurry: a **lollipop**, a **pick ax**, a **tube of toothpaste**, a **crescent moon**, a **balloon on a string**, a **vase**, an **umbrella**, a **drinking straw**, a **bird in flight**, a **fish**, a **coffee mug**, a **toothbrush**, and a **caterpillar**.

The sleeping leopard is too busy dreaming to care about these 17 objects: a **bunch of celery stalks,** a **crescent,** a **party horn, 2 thumbtacks,** a **cotton swab, 2 hearts,** a **hot dog,** a **carrot,** a **party hat,** a **lobster,** a **wristwatch,** a **hammer,** a **snow cone and straw,** a **hen,** and a **mushroom.**

Against the background of a slithering snake and tall trees you will discover the following 14 objects: a **handbag**, a **butterfly**, a **railroad spike**, a **strawberry**, a **makeup brush**, a **slingshot**, a **pen nib**, a **hockey stick**, a **tape measure**, a **bolt**, a **pair of lips**, a **spear**, a **parasol**, and an **olive fork**.

These gorillas are surrounded by 12 objects that don't concern them in the least: a **caveman's club**, a **lemon slice**, a **ratchet wrench**, a **comb**, a **map of Florida**, a **piece of birthday cake with candle**, a **mushroom**, a **bald eagle's head**, a **watermelon slice**, a **fish bone**, a **crowbar**, and an **antique musket**.

Eleven objects are concealed among the leaves where these orangutans are playing: a **pencil**, a **monkey wrench**, a **woodpecker**, an **apple**, a **bee**, a **quill pen**, a **pizza slice**, a **book**, a **hair bow**, a **fly**, and a **beetle**.

These cattle are grazing on the plains of our nation's
largest (continental) state. Find the hidden letters that
spell the name of this breed of Texas cattle.

Concealed in this picture of two towering giraffes are 14 objects: a
birthday candle, a **flashlight**, a **peanut**, an **alligator**, a **doughnut**,
a **crescent wrench**, a **dog bone**, a **flute**, a **door key**, a **pig's head**,
a **hairbrush**, a **U.S. map**, a **crab**, and a **mouse**.

Hidden among these kangaroos are the letters that spell the
name of the place where these delightful animals can be found.

Luckily for these chickens, the fox has decided not to make trouble in
the henhouse today. Look carefully at the fox and chickens and else-
where in the picture to locate the 15 concealed objects: a **hatchet**, a
shark, a **hammer**, a **baseball**, a **feather duster**, a **snow shovel**, a
pineapple, a **dog's name**, a **putty knife**, an **ice cream bar**,
a **shoe**, a **cracked egg**, a **shovel**, a **sailboat**, and a **frog**.

Bears certainly do like honey, as this picture reveals. The picture also contains 13 hidden objects: a **boxing glove**, a **tomahawk**, a **camera**, **2 carrots**, a **kite**, a **Christmas stocking**, a **tortoise**, a **coffee cup**, a **sawfish**, a **butter knife**, a **barbecue fork**, and a **dragon**.

This owl wants to know "who-o-o" has hidden these 12 objects in the picture: a **pair of scissors**, an **eraser**, a **glove**, a **shoe**, a **pair of pliers**, a **trophy**, a **toast slice**, a **fishing rod and reel**, an **apple**, a **marching band hat**, a **thumbtack**, and a **bugle**.

These lions are on the lookout for prey, but they haven't noticed the 11 objects hidden in the picture: an **ice cream bar**, a **clothespin**, a **snail**, a **teddy bear**, a **puppy**, a **running shoe**, an **ear of corn**, a **spool of thread**, a **spatula**, a **hairpin**, and a **witch's hat**.

If the elephants took a break from their bath, they might discover the following 11 objects: a **pony**, a **ruler**, a **diamond ring**, a **work glove**, a **hand mirror**, an **iron**, a **whisk broom**, an **ice cream cone**, a **crown**, a **fried egg**, and a **ballpoint pen**.

You would think that these wide-eyed birds would have spotted the 14 things hidden in the picture by now. Find the following items: a **golf club**, an **inchworm**, a **light bulb**, a **dustpan**, a **ladder**, a **baby bottle**, a **flag**, a **musical note**, a **book**, a **thimble**, a **slice of cake**, a **measuring spoon**, a **badminton shuttlecock**, and a **lizard**.

These butterflies are an amazing sight as they flutter about.
Look carefully and you will be able to find the following
14 things hidden among them: a **metal screw,** a **trowel,**
a **matador's hat,** a **needle,** a **dragonfly,** a **soup ladle,**
an **orange slice,** a **mop,** a **drawing pen,** a **slice of cake,**
a **pen knife,** a **crescent moon,** a **maraca,** and a **bottle.**

Watch your step! If these tiny insects were to sting you,
you might react with the words **OUCH! FIRE ANTS!**
Now look carefully at this picture to find the letters
and punctuation for these words.

This diver found more than a shipwreck in the ocean. He also saw the following 23 objects: a **spoon,** a **fork,** a **rat,** a **bowling pin,** a **car key,** a **saucepan,** a **handbag,** an **acorn,** a **turtle,** a **crayon,** a **map of Texas,** a **toothbrush,** a **shoe,** an **ice cream pop,** a **mitten,** a **mallet,** a **dove,** a **hatchet,** a **sewing needle,** an **artist's paintbrush,** a **fried egg,** a **pizza slice,** and a **fishhook.**

Solutions

page 1

page 2

page 3

page 4

page 5

page 6

page 7

page 8

page 9

page 10

page 11

page 12

LONGHORNS
page 13

page 14

AUSTRALIA
page 15

page 16

page 17

page 18

page 19

page 20

page 21

page 22

page 23

page 24

HIDDEN PICTURE
CHALLENGE

Stephen Stanley

PUBLISHER'S NOTE

Appearances can be deceiving. Each of the 24 drawings in this book has a number of everyday objects hidden within it. The items to be found are listed below each picture. Look carefully though, these puzzles are a real challenge! Solutions are given starting on page 57.

Shopping list

The last place Mrs. Robertson expected to find the **8 items on her shopping list** was in the "Funny Masks" section of her local supermarket.

It is Jake's birthday party, but the birthday cake seems to have disappeared. Can you spot **8 slices of birthday cake** and **1 cupcake** for Jake?

Happy landings! The passengers will need a **suitcase**, a **book**, **sunglasses**, a **camcorder**, a **passport**, a **cassette player**, a **postcard**, an **umbrella**, and a **carry-on bag** to make their trip more comfortable.

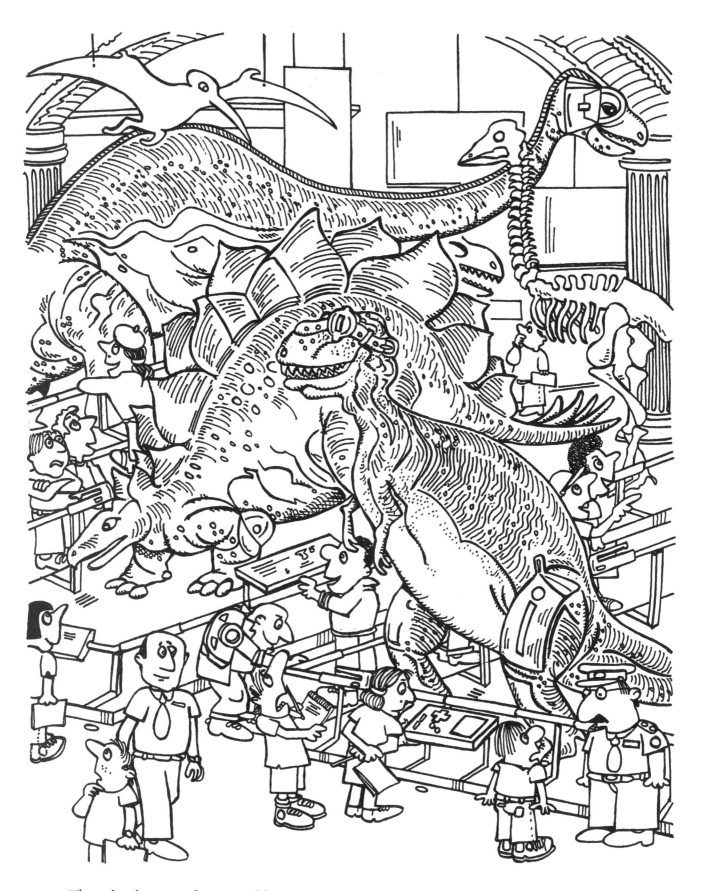

The school visit to the natural history museum went well, except that the children lost a
watch, a **purse**, a **camera**, a **notepad**, a **book**, a **pencil case**, a **cap**, a
video game, and **3 pens**.

Tim and Robin have stumbled across a spaceship in the woods. It looks deserted, but they are being watched by **12 aliens**.

You'd be amazed at the things taken into orbit by the Space Shuttle these days: a **key**, an **elephant**, a **bunch of flowers**, a **vase**, a **toothbrush**, a **turtle**, a **can opener**, a **car tire**, and a **pair of ballet shoes**.

The boys will need uniforms if they decide to form a team. Although they don't know it, they already have the **numbers 1–9** around them.

Even in the middle of winter you can find some reminders of summer—a **bottle of sunscreen**, a **straw hat**, an **ice cream cone**, a **popsicle**, a **pair of sunglasses**, a **cool drink**, a **pair of shorts**, and the **sun**.

The local shoe store has just opened every shoe box in the shop and discovered they contain not a single shoe! Can you find the **9 shoes** hidden in the store somewhere?

When the class visited a TV studio, they were told to stay very quiet; but there were some very noisy things in the studio: a **whistle**, a **drum**, an **alarm clock**, a **horn**, a **jet aircraft**, a **frog**, a **bullhorn**, a **firecracker**, and a **bell**.

The children could think of lots more exciting ways of getting to school each day than taking the bus or riding their bikes, such as by **parachute**, by **car**, on **horseback**, by **helicopter**, by **sailboat**, by **motorcycle**, by **balloon**, by **jet aircraft**, or by **rocket**.

Camping out is fun, but sometime even happy campers dream of the comforts of home, such as: **television**, a **soft bed**, a **bathtub**, a **faucet handle**, an **armchair**, a **microwave oven**, a **kettle**, a **lamp**, and an **electric plug**.

The parade starts in five minutes and the band can't find their instruments. Can you find a **trumpet**, a **saxophone**, a **tuba**, a **trombone**, a **French horn**, a **drum**, **cymbals**, a **triangle**, and a **baton**?

Oh, no! Bill has just dropped and broken his video game and has lost **9 characters** from the game he was playing. Can you find them?

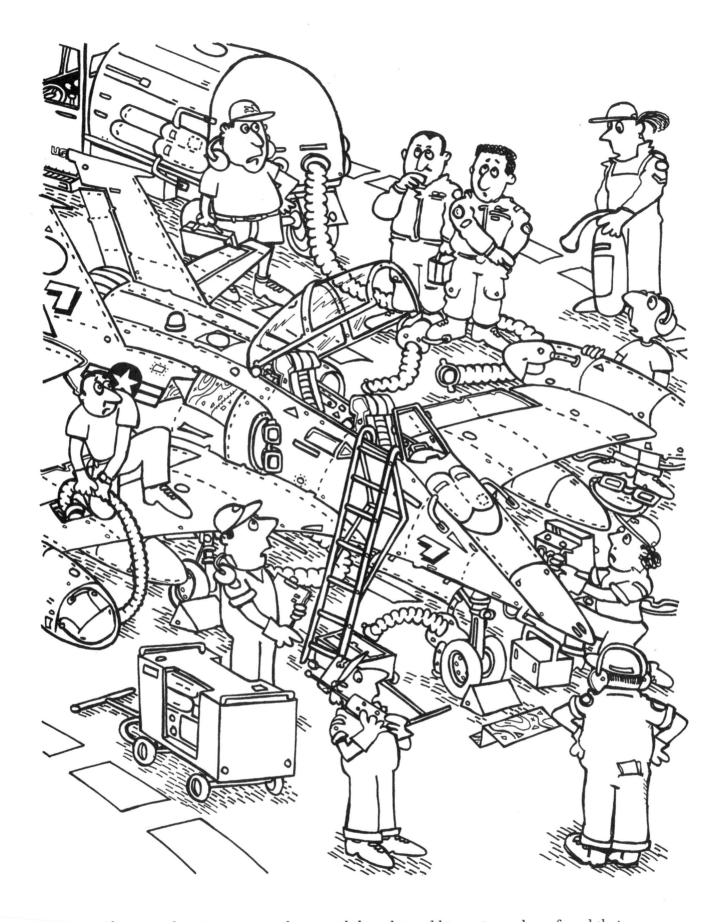

This aircraft isn't going anywhere until the pilot and his navigator have found their
helmets, **goggles**, **oxygen masks**, **life jackets**, and **maps**.

When the school visited the zoo, the children expected to see some animals, but perhaps the animals were just shy. Can you see a **hyena**, a **chameleon**, a **giant panda**, a **crocodile**, a **flamingo**, a **crane**, a **koala**, a **zebra**, and a **toucan**?

The concert is about to begin, but the band has lost its music. Can you find **11 single notes, 2 pairs of notes,** and **2 triplets**?

Just which sport are these spectators watching? Can you find a **basketball**, a **football**, a **soccer ball**, a **golf club**, a **tennis racquet**, a **baseball bat**, a **hockey stick**, a **motorcycle**, and weight lifters' **dumbbells**?

Can you help the workers in this laboratory discover
14 new and different **types of bug**?

All **8** members of the famous Ziferelli acrobatic troupe have lost the letter "**Z**" from the front and back of their uniforms.

How can you spend a day at sea and not see anything? Help the crew to find a **dolphin**, a **lobster**, a **shark**, a **sea horse**, a **swordfish**, a **manta ray**, a **crab**, a **jellyfish**, **6 smaller fish,** and a **very tiny whale**.

The old west was a very windy place. Here are **7** cowhands who have each lost their **hats** in the wind.

Witch Wanda has invited her ghoulish guests to a Halloween party at Castle Cobweb, but everyone is terrified to discover that the castle is "haunted" by **8 ordinary humans**.

It is Christmas Eve, and only the dog Molly knows where Santa has left the presents: a
teddy bear, a **bicycle**, a **radio-controlled car** and its **controller**, a **book**, a
robot, a **doll**, and a **CD**.

SOLUTIONS

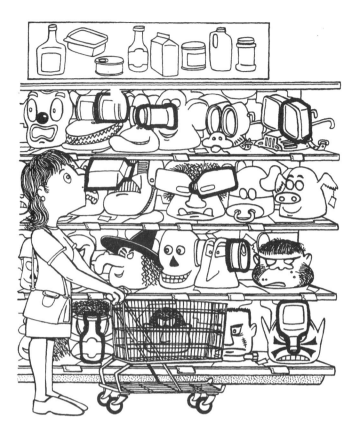

page 33

page 34

page 35

page 36

page 37

page 38

page 39

page 40

page 41

page 42

page 43

page 44

page 45

page 46

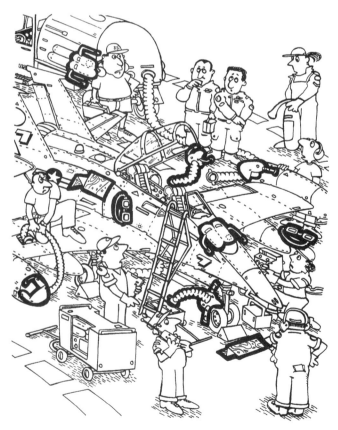

page 47

page 48

page 49

page 50

page 51

page 52

page 53

page 54

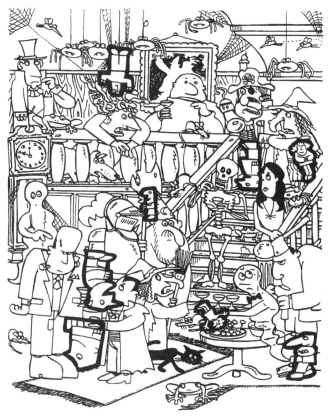

page 55

page 56

THE
ULTIMATE
HIDDEN PICTURE
PUZZLE BOOK

Joe Boddy

PUBLISHER'S NOTE

This is a collection of puzzles that have hidden elements (such as letters, animals, and household utensils) that you must try to discover. Captions beneath each drawing tell you what to look for and in what quantity. Look very carefully for each hidden item before checking the answers in the back of the book. For even more fun, every drawing in this book is perfect for coloring in any way you like. You can either color the hidden objects you find to make them stand out or leave them "hidden" so your friends also can try to solve these challenging puzzles.

Andrew is deep in the rain forest. But he isn't worried because he knows that if he looks closely he will find all the things he needs: **a fishing pole, a frying pan, a book of matches, hiking boots, a turtleneck sweater, a jackknife, a tent,** and **a compass** to show him the way home.

Zara has just realized that her magic spell is not going to work—she has forgotten the magic word. You know that word, so you must help her find it. There are 6 hidden letters: **L, A, S, P,** and **2 E's.** Find them and put them in the right order and you will have the magic word.

Amy and her bird friend Yma are the best tree-house builders in town. Amy has one problem though—she never puts her tools away and so she keeps losing them. Can you help her find them? They are: **a tape measure, a screwdriver, a power drill, needlenose pliers, 5 nails, a hammer, a saw,** and **a lunch box.**

It's always fun to go shopping downtown. And it's even more fun to find a couple of "bargains." Look closely and you will find **2 B's, 4 A's, 2 R's, 2 G's, 2 I's,** and **2 N's.**

Freya's favorite fishing hole is well stocked with excitement. There are **12 fish** bigger than the one she's caught. In addition, for even *more* excitement she might catch **a shark** and **a whale**. Can you find them all?

Big Hans is not the mean giant everybody thinks he is. He has simply misplaced his glasses. Help him find his **mug, spoon, fork, axe, hand broom, candle, needle,** and **spool of thread.** You'd save this village a lot of trouble if you were to find his **glasses** too.

Lance has just returned from a long day of dragon hunting. He is looking forward to **a bowl of soup, a piece of cheese, a hot bath, a toothbrush, a big comfy chair, a pair of slippers,** and **a good book.** Can you help him find everything he needs?

Poor Jess—the only thing he can find to eat is a plate of cookies. The cupboard is empty . . . or is it? Try to find these other things to eat: **a banana, an apple, a cracker, a hamburger, a hot dog, a carton of milk, a fish, a celery bunch, 2 eggs, a slice of bread, an ear of corn, a piece of cheese,** and **a can of beans.**

Just an old house on Halloween night?
Keep your eyes open—look left and look right.
You'll see **the witch's face,** her **broom** and **cooking pot,**
Her **bat** and **cat,** her **skull** and **hat,** and **gravestone plot.**
Find all these and a **ghostie** too,
And you won't be afraid if he hollers "Boo!"

73

There are always many interesting characters to be found downtown. Can you find 12 characters of the alphabet for yourself?—**Z, V, C, F, L, E, S, R, U, O, Y.** And can you find "yourself"?

Jan is in the middle of a forest looking for a place to camp. She doesn't realize that this enchanted wood has **a house, bed, table, chair, cup, fork,** and **spoon** all ready for her comfort. Can you find them?

Debbie has found the dragon that had stolen various items from her family. Can she find her mother's **teapot** and **cup**? Her father's **hammer**? Her brother's **bat** and **ball**? Can she tiptoe in and get her **lamp, comb,** and **teddy bear** before the dragon wakes up? Maybe you can help.

Pedro has a very hard working road crew and they get very hungry by lunchtime. Now it's time to eat and he has to find his **lunch box, a banana, a wedge of cheese, a carrot, 2 apples, an ice cream cone, 6 sandwiches, a thermos,** and **a cup.** Can you help him?

Most of the rats just aren't cooperating with the Pied Piper. Can you find the only **one** that is following him, and the other **8 rats** that are in hiding?

Marty is a messy mechanic. He's lost his **screwdriver** and **flashlight** in this clutter. He's misplaced **the steering wheel, the instruction book, the car key,** and, worst of all, **the name of the man** who owns the car. Can you be of assistance? (Bonus: see if you can locate these auto parts—*radiator, muffler, spark plug, transmission, gas can,* and *battery.*)

Sam has come across a very unusual treasure ship. He won't find any old gold coins or silver bars, but with your help he may find a new **television, headphones, a telephone receiver, a bottle of soda, a skateboard,** and **a camera.** You might want to hurry, though, that shark is looking pretty hungry.

If you are planning a train ride to Grandma's house, don't forget your **suitcase, toothbrush, toothpaste, comb, hand mirror, a book** to read on the way, and **a dime** to call her when you arrive. Can you locate these necessities before it's time to go?

The hay is in and the corn is ready. All Matilda and Max need now are the animals to feed. Can you help them find **5 farm creatures** that eat hay or corn?

It's not much fun having to stay after school just because you can't find your things. Can you help Matt find his things? They are: his **book, folder, lunch box, pencil, ballpoint pen, eraser,** and **writing pad.**

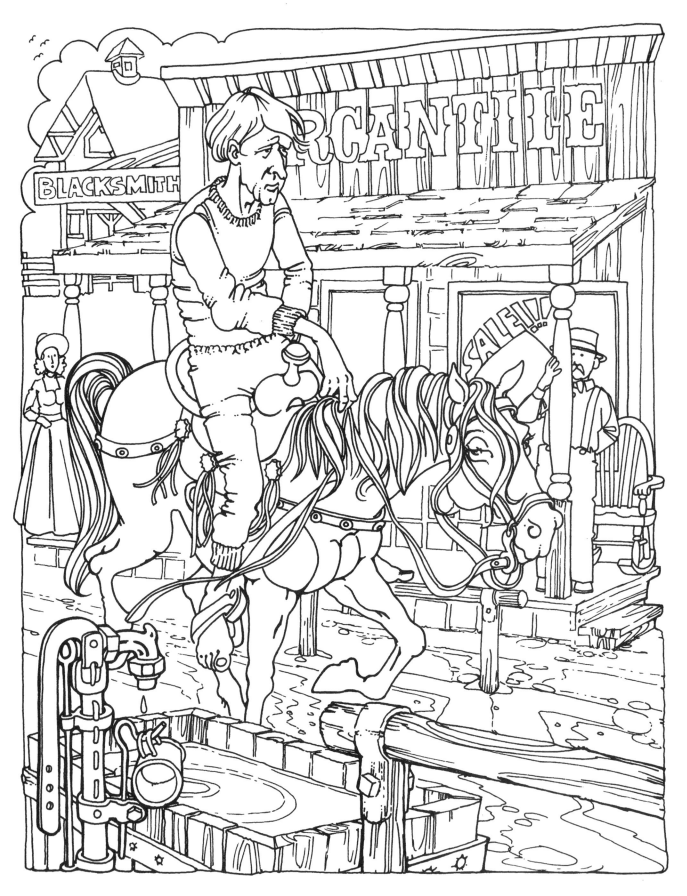

This cowboy has come to town for the big sale. He wants to buy some much needed clothing. Since you know this town better than he does help him locate **2 boots, pants, a belt, a sock, a shirt, a T-shirt,** and, of course, **a cowboy hat.**

Brant is not *just* a little frog in a big pond. He's also a world explorer with his own **jet plane**, **boat**, **2 paddles**, **face mask**, **backpack**, **machete**, and **binoculars**. Don't believe it? See for yourself.

Rodolphe the repairman is a creative genius. He'll get this place fixed up as soon as you help him find the following: his **hammer, 2 nails, paint can, paint roller, paintbrush, putty knife,** and **ladder.**

Freddy grows the best fruit in the county. The only problem is finding it all. Can you help our friend find **14 apples, 4 strawberries, 3 pears, 2 cherries, a lemon, 3 bananas,** and **a bunch of grapes**?

It's obvious that Manfred the monkey has a whole jungle full of friends. Since he can't count he doesn't know how many friends he has. Can you count them for him?

SOLUTIONS

page 65

The magic word is **PLEASE**.

page 66

page 67

page 68

page 69

page 70

page 71

page 72

page 73

"Yourself" is made up of the last 8 hidden letters.
page 74

page 75

page 76

page 77

page 78

page 79

page 80

page 81

page 82

page 83

page 84

page 85

page 86

page 87

Manfred has 27 friends.
page 88